Footloose the stage musical

T0088326

Songbook and CD Artwork by Frank "Fraver" Verlizzo.
© 2011 Rodgers & Hammerstein: An Imagem Company.

ISBN 978-1-4584-1615-5

HAL•LEONARD®
CORPORATION
7777 W. BLUEMOUND RD. P.O. BOX 13819 MILWAUKEE, WI 53213

In Australia Contact:
Hal Leonard Australia Pty. Ltd.
4 Lentara Court
Cheltenham, Victoria, 3192 Australia
Email: ausadmin@halleonard.com.au

Visit Hal Leonard Online at
www.halleonard.com

ALMOST PARADISE

Words by DEAN PITCHFORD
Music by ERIC CARMEN

Moderately slow Rock Ballad

REN:

I thought that dreams be-longed to oth-er men,   'cause

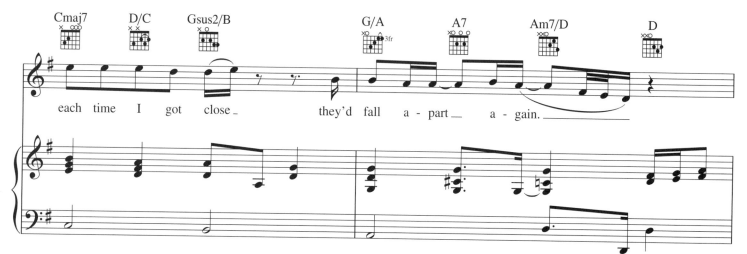

each time I got close ___ they'd fall a-part ___ a - gain. ___

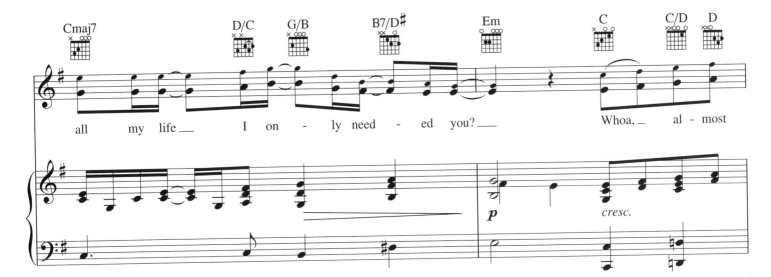

par - a - dise; _____ how could we ask __ for _____ more? I

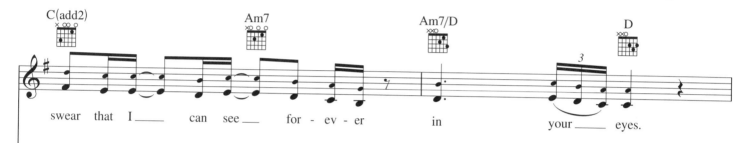

swear that I ___ can see __ for - ev - er in your ___ eyes.

Par - a - dise. __

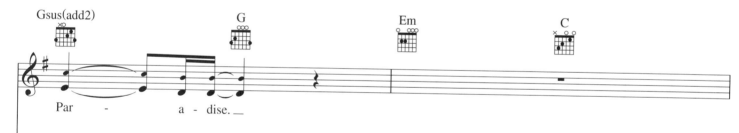

ARIEL:

I thought that per - fect love __ was hard to find. I'd

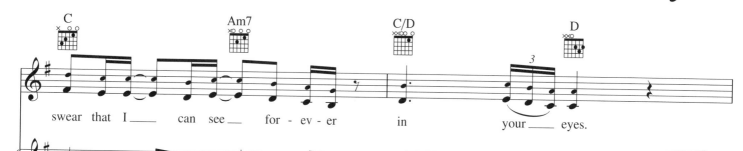

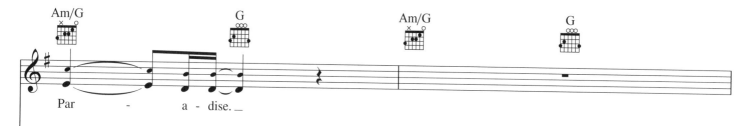

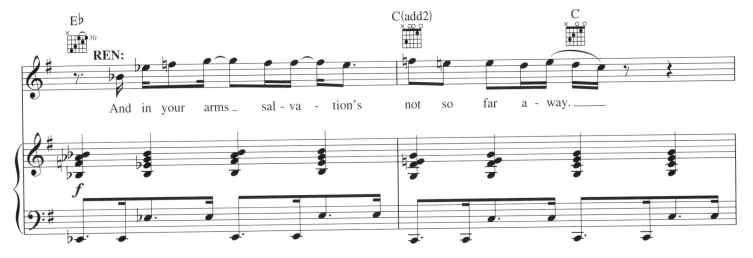

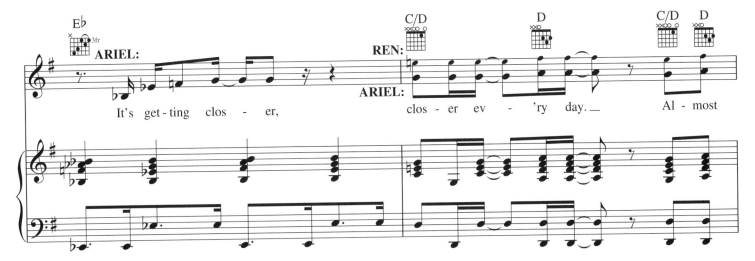

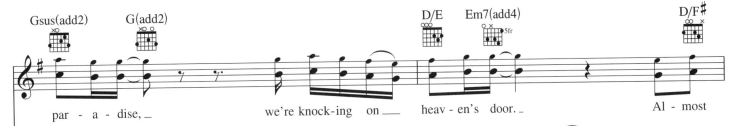

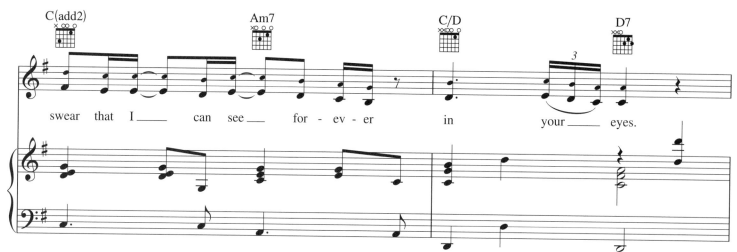

swear that I ____ can see ____ for - ev - er in your ____ eyes.

Par - a - dise. ____

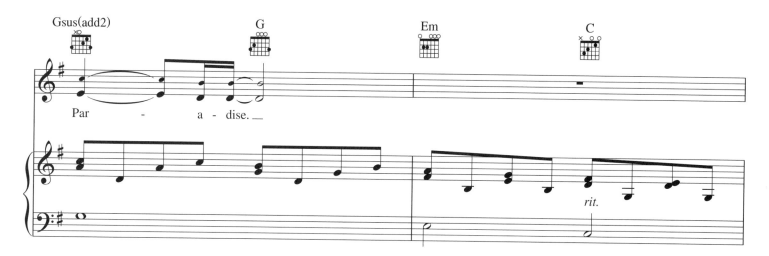

Par - a - dise. ____

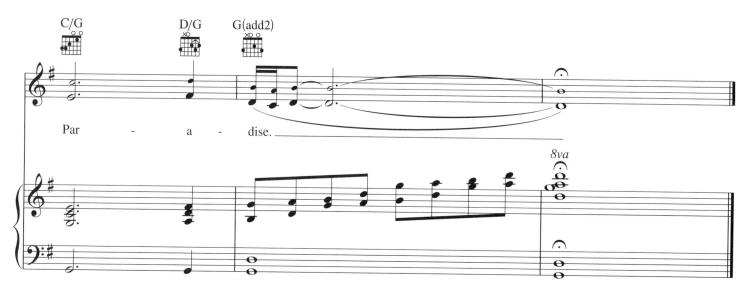

Par - a - dise. ____

CAN YOU FIND IT IN YOUR HEART?

Words by DEAN PITCHFORD
Music by TOM SNOW

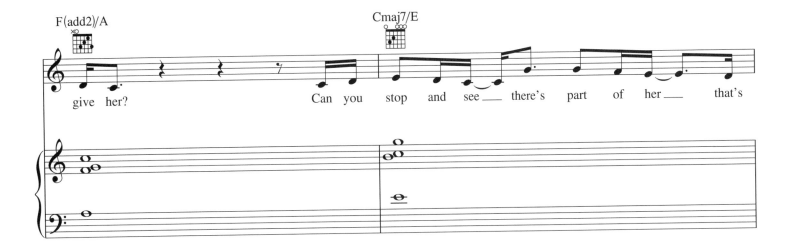

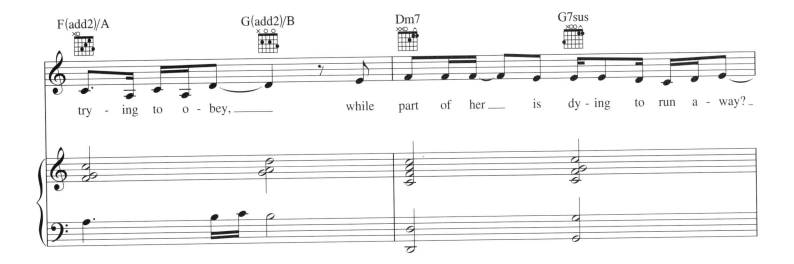

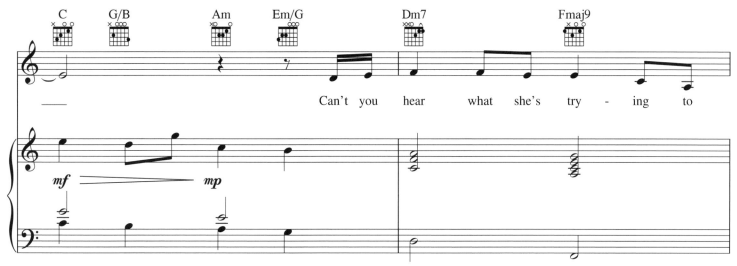

Can't you hear what she's try - ing to

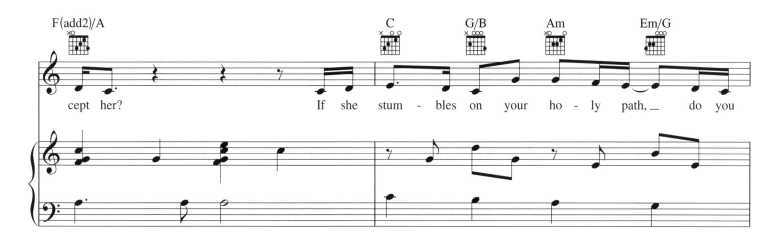

Moderately

say? ___ Can you find it in ___ your soul ___ to ac -

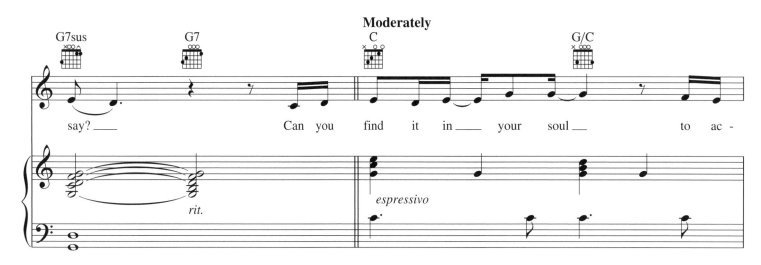

cept her? If she stum - bles on your ho - ly path, ___ do you

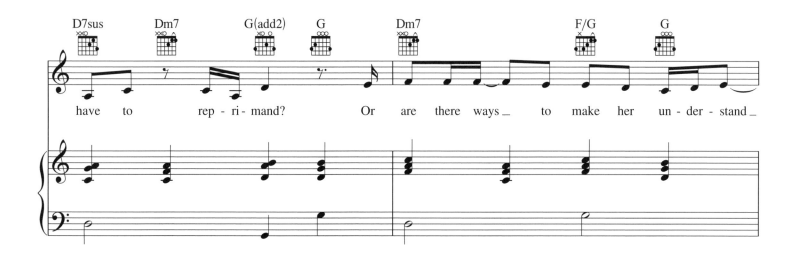

have to rep - ri - mand? Or are there ways ___ to make her un - der - stand ___

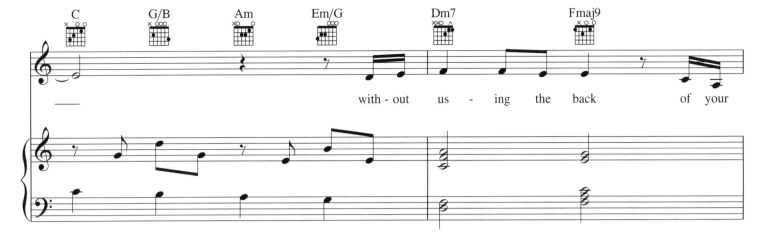

with - out us - ing the back of your

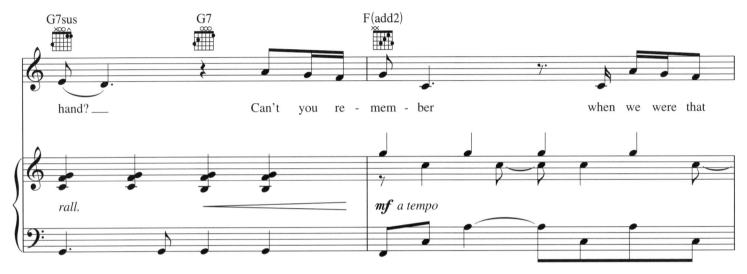

hand? ___ Can't you re - mem - ber when we were that

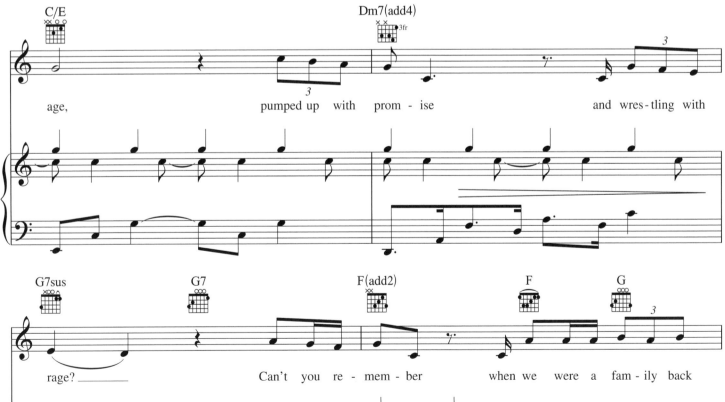

age, pumped up with prom - ise and wres - tling with

rage? ___ Can't you re - mem - ber when we were a fam - ily back

when? Could we be one a - gain?

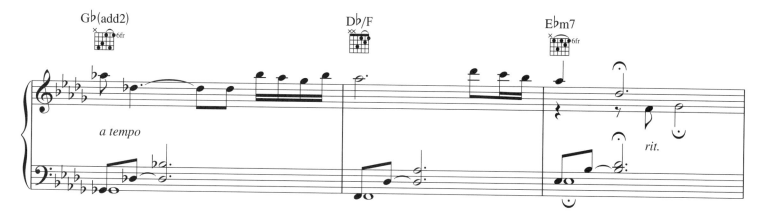

a tempo

rit.

Does it ev - er cross_ your mind_ that I

a tempo

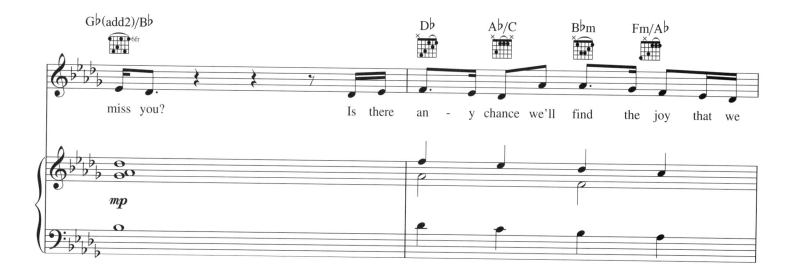

miss you? Is there an - y chance we'll find the joy that we

FOOTLOOSE

Words by DEAN PITCHFORD
Music by KENNY LOGGINS

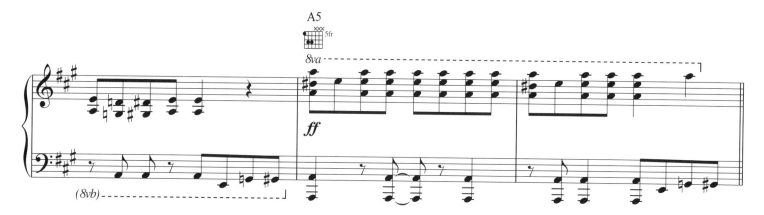

This edition may be sung by a solo singer. The song appears in a different form in the show, accommodating various singers' entrances.

my __ card.　　Eight ho - urs,　　for what?　　Oh, tell me

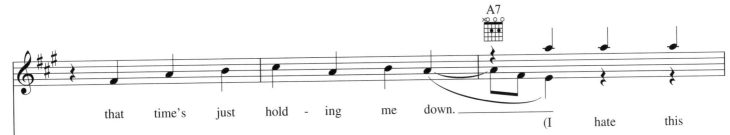

what I got.　　I got this feel - ing __

that time's just hold - ing me down. _____ (I hate this

feel - ing; time is hold - ing me down.) __

I'll hit the ceil - ing, ___ or else I'll

tear up this town. ___

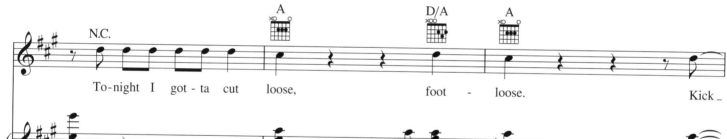

To-night I got-ta cut loose, foot - loose. Kick

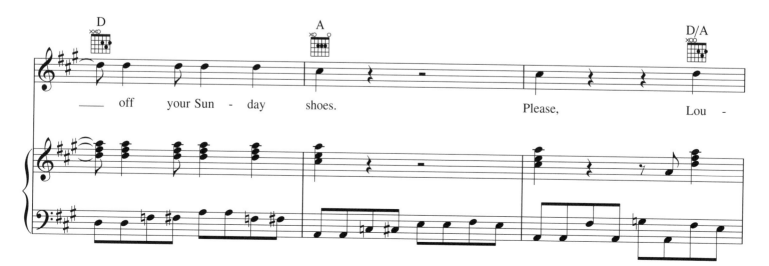

___ off your Sun - day shoes. Please, Lou -

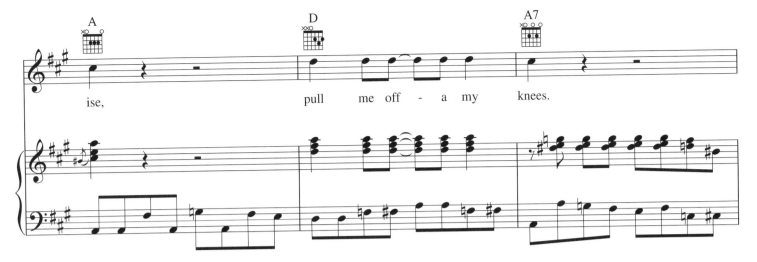

ise,   pull   me   off - a   my   knees.

Jack,   get   back,   come __ on _____ be -

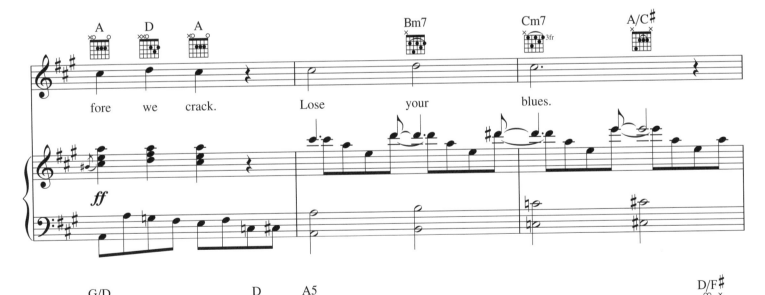

fore   we   crack.   Lose   your   blues.

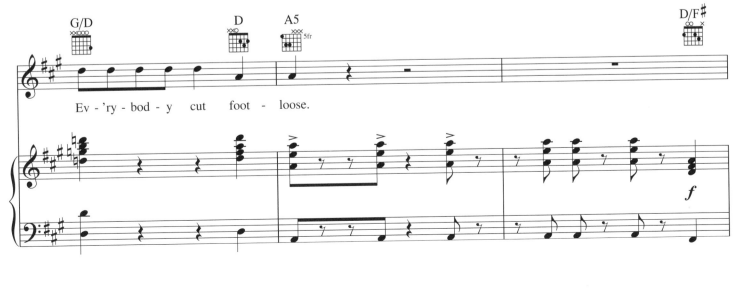

Ev - 'ry - bod - y   cut   foot - loose.

You're play-in' so ___ cool, o-bey-in'

ev-er-y rule. Dig way down in your ___ heart.

You're burn-in', yearn-in' for some, some-bod-y to

tell you ___ that life ain't pass-in' you by. ___

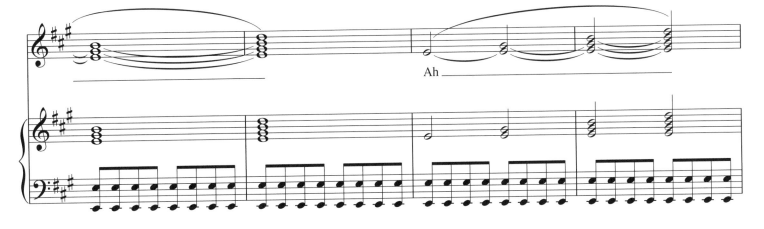

Ah

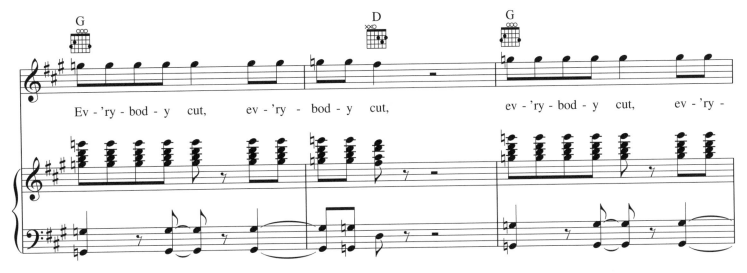

Ev -'ry - bod - y cut, ev -'ry - bod - y cut, ev -'ry - bod - y cut, ev -'ry -

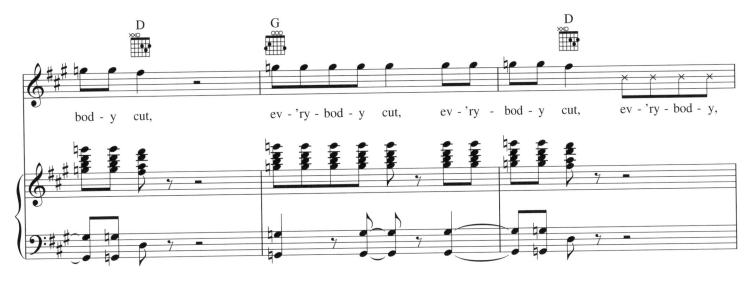

bod - y cut, ev -'ry - bod - y cut, ev -'ry - bod - y cut, ev -'ry - bod - y,

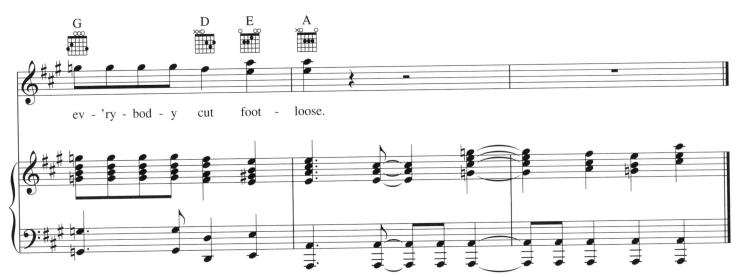

ev -'ry - bod - y cut foot - loose.

THE GIRL GETS AROUND

Words by DEAN PITCHFORD
Music by SAMMY HAGAR

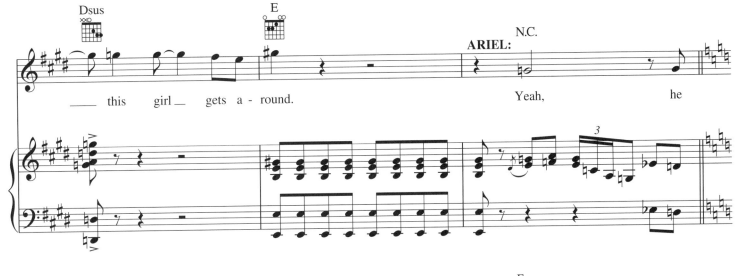

this girl ___ gets a - round. Yeah, he

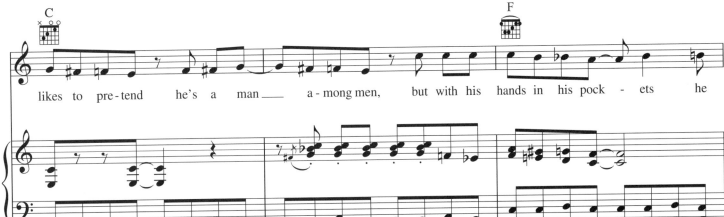

likes to pre-tend he's a man ___ a-mong men, but with his hands in his pock - ets he

can't count to ten. ___ Don't wor-ry, ba - by, your se - cret's safe with

me. And he bores ___ me to tears ___ with his beers ___

and his bikes, but I keep him a - round _ 'cause when temp - ta - tion strikes, _

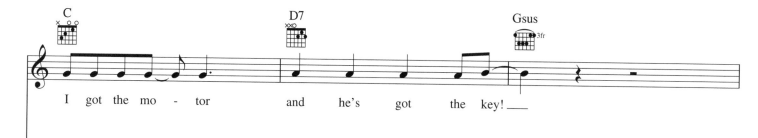

I got the mo - tor and he's got the key! _

CHUCK:
The girl gets a - round. _____ She

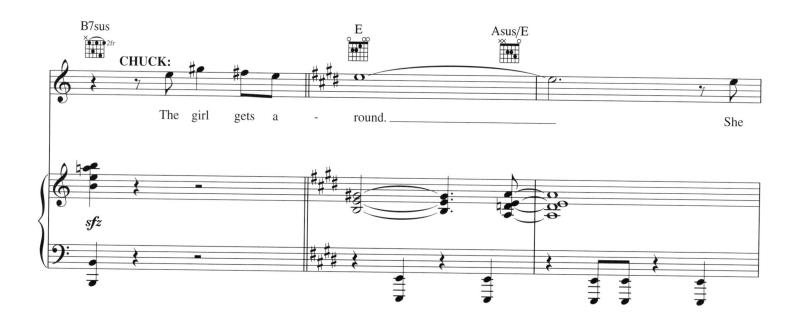

LEARNING TO BE SILENT

Words by DEAN PITCHFORD
Music by TOM SNOW

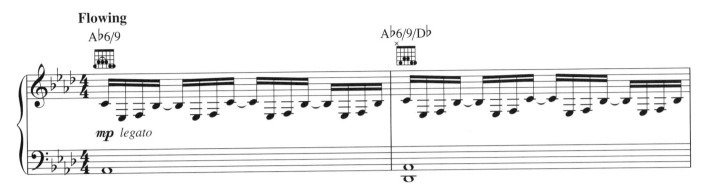

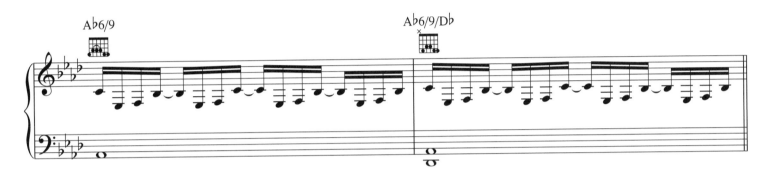

Swal-low-ing my words, _____ star-ing at the floor, _____

count-ing lit-tle cracks in the tile, strug-gl-ing to smile with out chok-ing, learn-ing to be

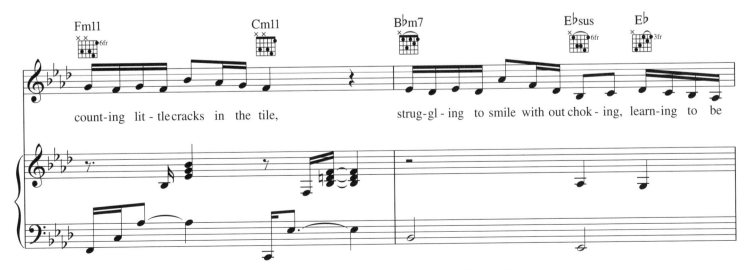

HEAVEN HELP ME

Words by DEAN PITCHFORD
Music by TOM SNOW

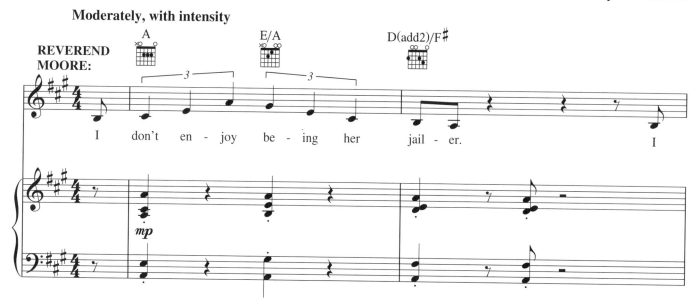

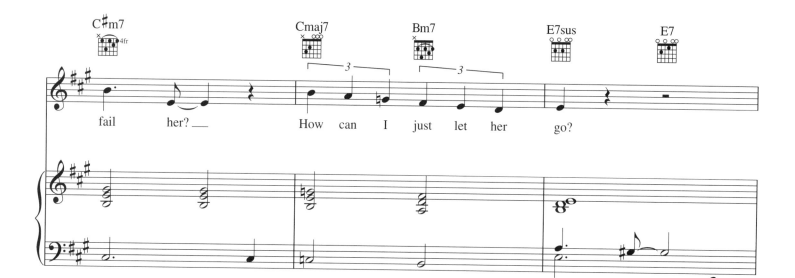

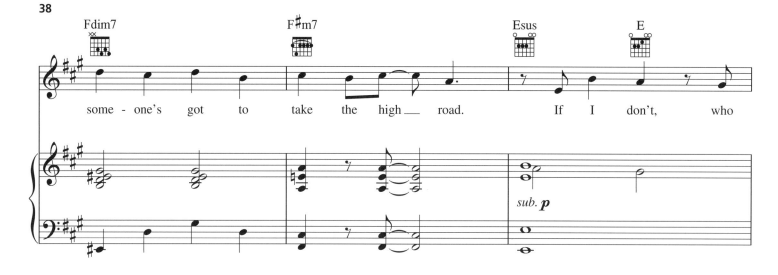

some-one's got to take the high ___ road. If I don't, who

will? I be-came ___ a man of God ___

to do His work, to spread His word, to ease some pain and

dry some tears. That was the plan. But

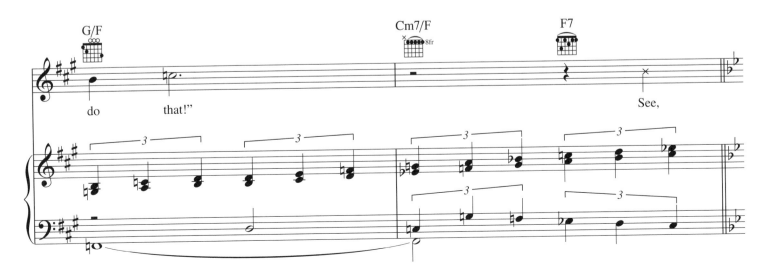

save his fam-'ly and his neigh-bors? Heav- en

help me. Oh, Heav-en help me. __

If Heav-en can't, _____ who

can? _____

HOLDING OUT FOR A HERO

Words by DEAN PITCHFORD
Music by JIM STEINMAN

knight up-on a fi - ery steed?

Late at night I toss and I turn (I toss and I turn, ooh.)

and I dream of what I need. I need a

Disco Appassionato

he - ro! (Doo doo doo

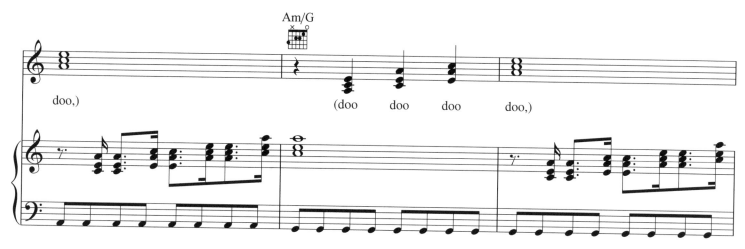

doo,) (doo doo doo doo,)

(doo doo doo doo.) (Ahh!

Ahh!) Some-where af - ter mid - night, in my

wild - est fan - tas - y,_____ some - where just _ be - yond _

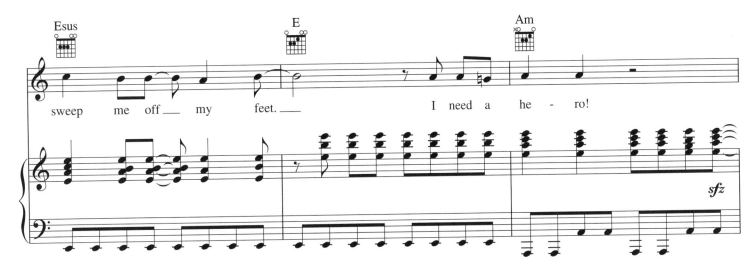

-ta be soon,_ and he's got - ta be larg - er than life._____ Larg - er than

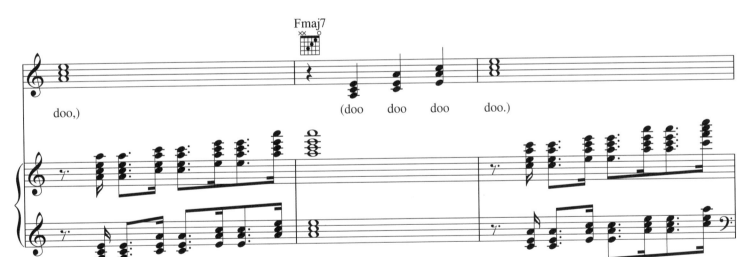

life! _____ (Doo doo doo doo,)   (doo doo doo

doo,)   (doo doo doo doo.)

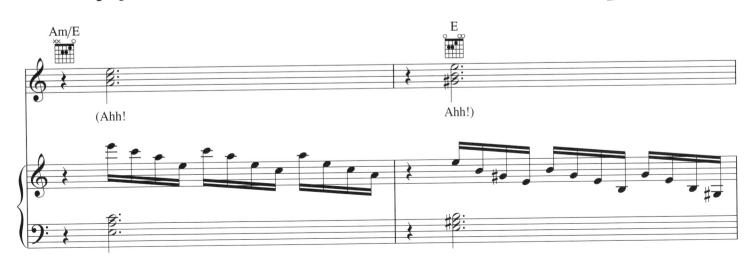

(Ahh!   Ahh!)

Up where the moun-tains meet the heav-ens a - bove, ___

out where the light-ning splits ___ the sea, _____ I could swear ___ there is some-

- one, some - where, watch - ing me. _____

Through the wind ___ and the chill ___ and the rain, ___ and the storm ___ and the flood, ___

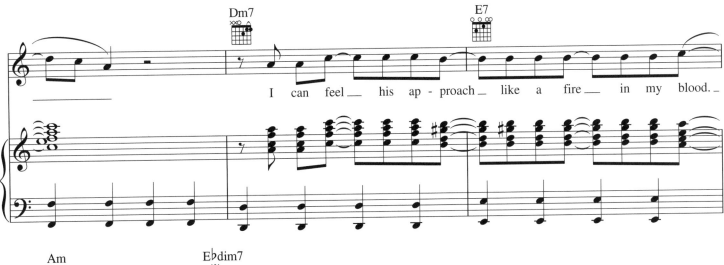

I can feel __ his ap - proach __ like a fire __ in my blood. __

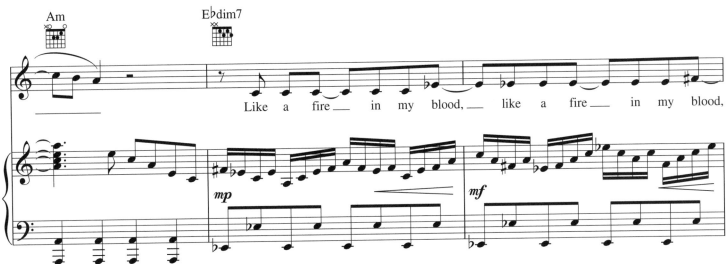

Like a fire __ in my blood, __ like a fire __ in my blood,

__ like a fire __ in my blood, __ like a fire __ in my...

Ahh! Ahh! I need a he - ro!

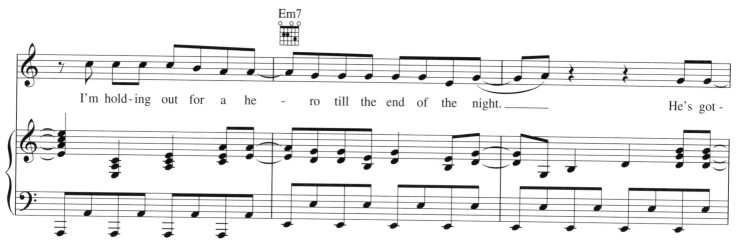

-ta be soon,__ and he's got-ta be larg-er than life._____ Larg-er than

life!_____ (Doo doo doo doo) (Doo doo doo

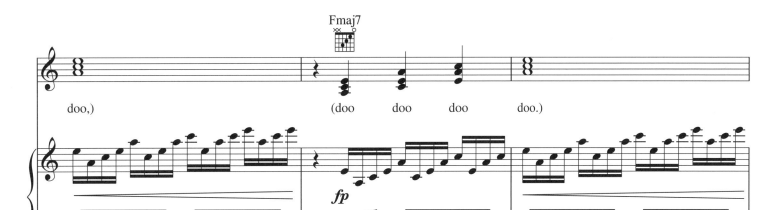

doo,) (doo doo doo doo.)

(Ahh! Ahh!) I need a he-ro!

I CAN'T STAND STILL

Words by DEAN PITCHFORD
Music by TOM SNOW

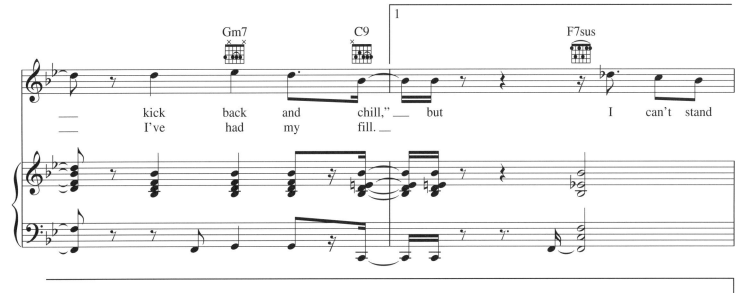

kick back and chill," but I can't stand
I've had my fill.

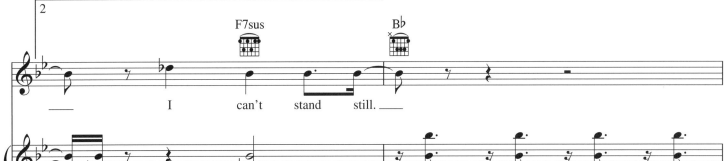

still!

I can't stand still.

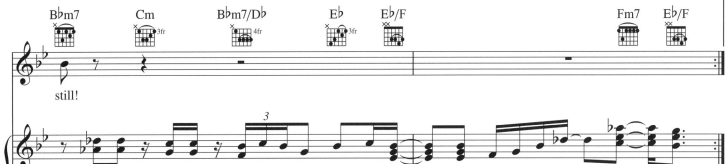

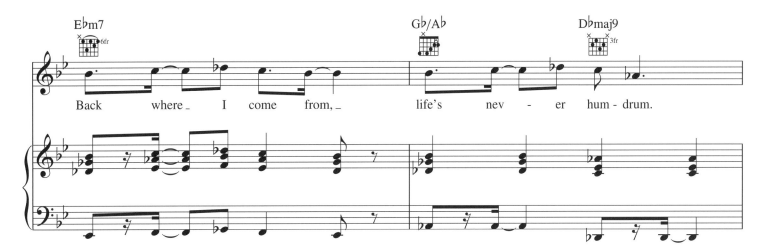

Back where I come from, life's nev-er hum-drum.

I wish _ I ___ could take _ you there. ___ Oh, _____

___ we had the world at our feet. Life was

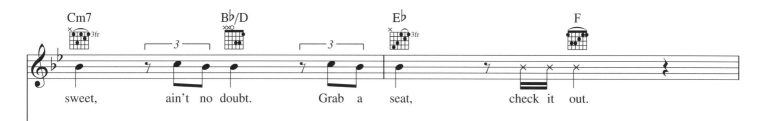

sweet, ain't no doubt. Grab a seat, check it out.

Oh,   I thought it nev - er would end. _____   But I

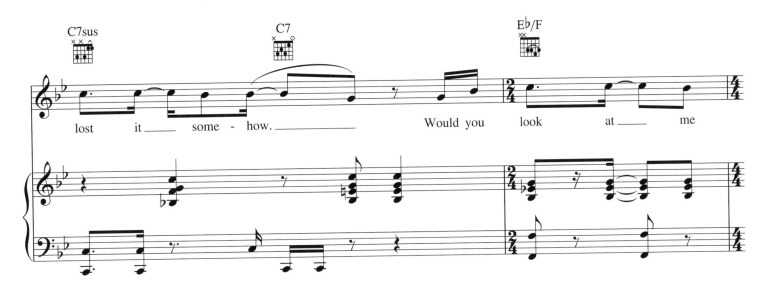

lost it ____ some - how. _____   Would you   look   at ____ me

now? _____   I'm try - in' hard _ to tone _ it down. _

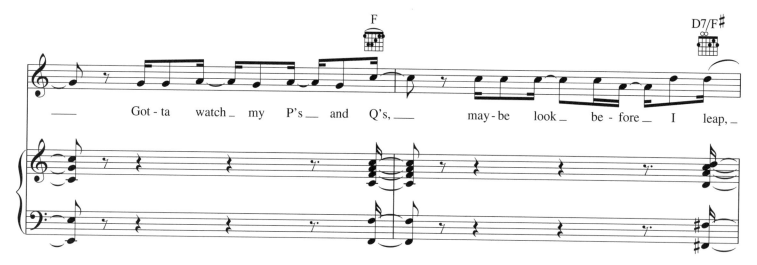

Got - ta watch _ my P's _ and Q's, _ may-be look _ be - fore _ I leap, _

_ and then I think, _ "Hey, what's the use?" _ Ain't done it yet, _

_ and I can't for - get how it feels when you dance till you drop, so

don't e - ven start to sug-gest that I stop. I nev - er

I'M FREE
(Heaven Helps the Man)

Words by DEAN PITCHFORD
Music by KENNY LOGGINS

Quickly, intense

REN:

Look-ing in-to your eyes, I know I'm right. _____
Run-ning a-way will nev-er make you free; _____

If there's an-y-thing worth a fear, it's worth a
It does-n't mat-ter where you go, I ___ guar-an-

fight. ___
tee. ___

No ___ one can tie my
Long ___ as we hold our ___

hands or make me change my plans. ___
ground we can-not be bound. ___

I'm cross-
We're shak-

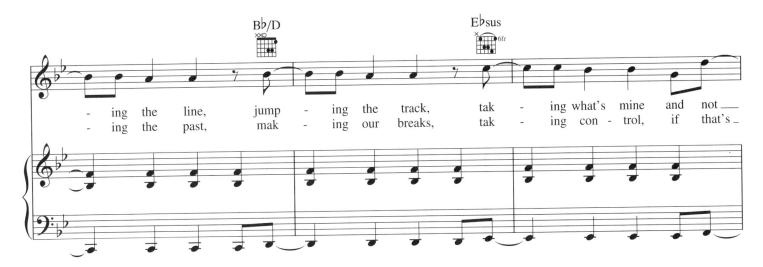

- ing the line, jump - ing the track, tak - ing what's mine and not ___
- ing the past, mak - ing our breaks, tak - ing con - trol, if that's ___

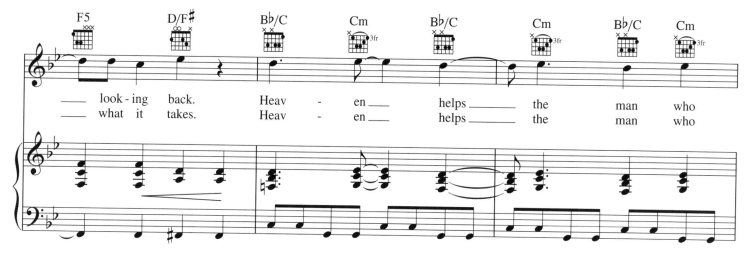

look - ing back. Heav - en ___ helps ___ the man who
what it takes. Heav - en ___ helps ___ the man who

fights his ___ fear; ___ ev - 'ry ___ day ___
fights his ___ fear; ___ we can ___ face ___

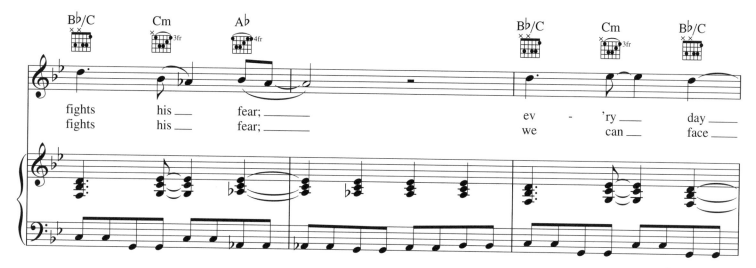

___ I face a new fron - tier. ___
___ it face down right now, right here. ___

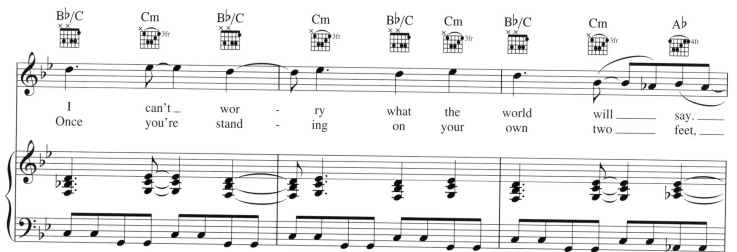

I can't ___ wor - ry what the world will ___ say. ___
Once you're stand - ing on your own two ___ feet, ___

I may __ fly __ or __ fall, but
you will __ not __ re - treat if

ei - ther way, _____ I'm free!
you re - peat: _____ I'm

free!   I'm   free!

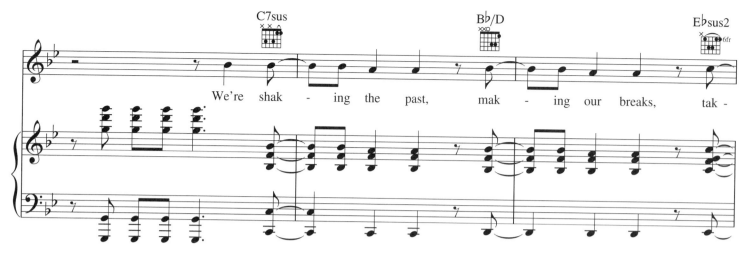

We're shak - ing the past, mak - ing our breaks, tak-

- ing con - trol, if that's ___ what it takes. Heav - en ___ helps ___

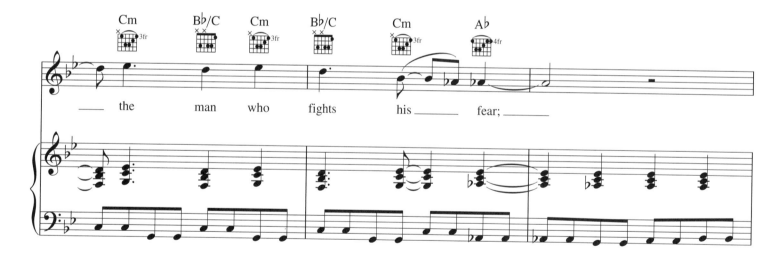

___ the man who fights his ___ fear; ___

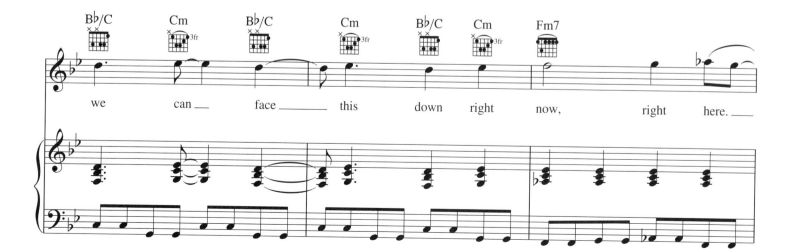

we can ___ face ___ this down right now, right here. ___

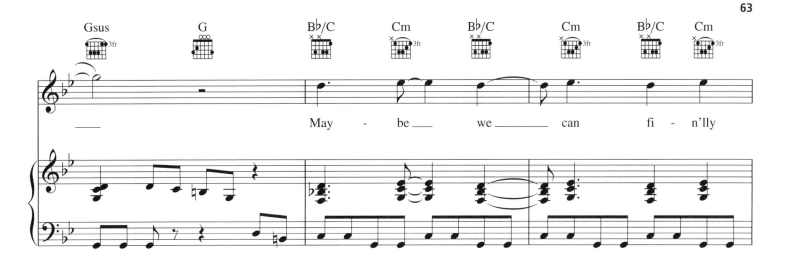

May - be ___ we ___ can fi - n'lly

right this ___ wrong. ___ Arm in ___ arm ___

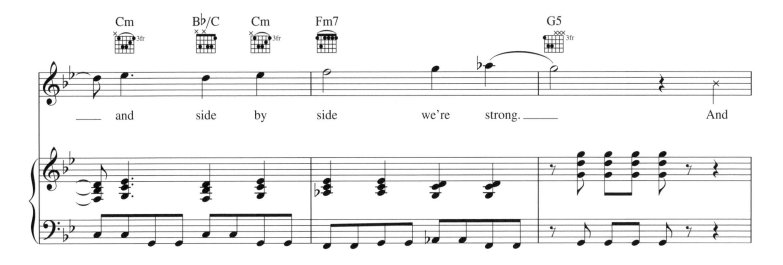

___ and side by side we're strong. ___ And

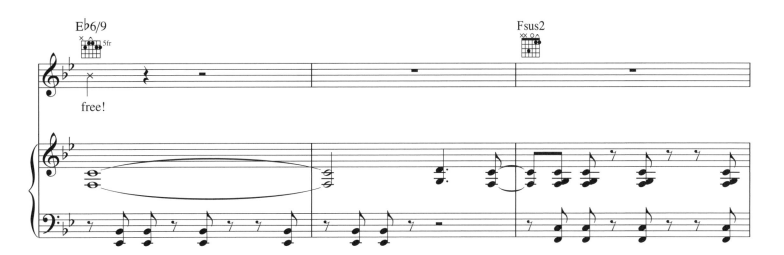

free!

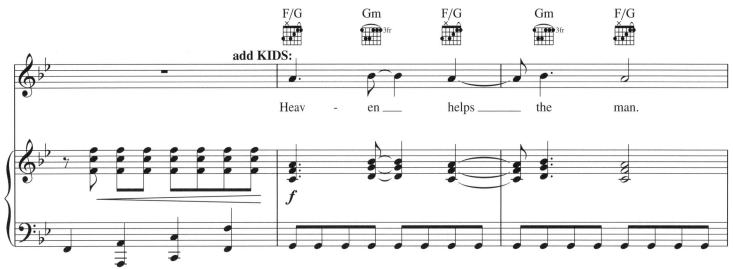

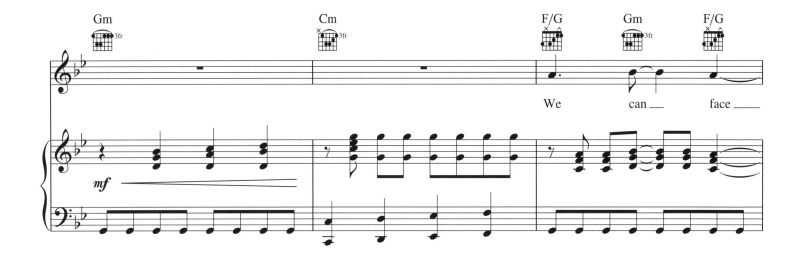

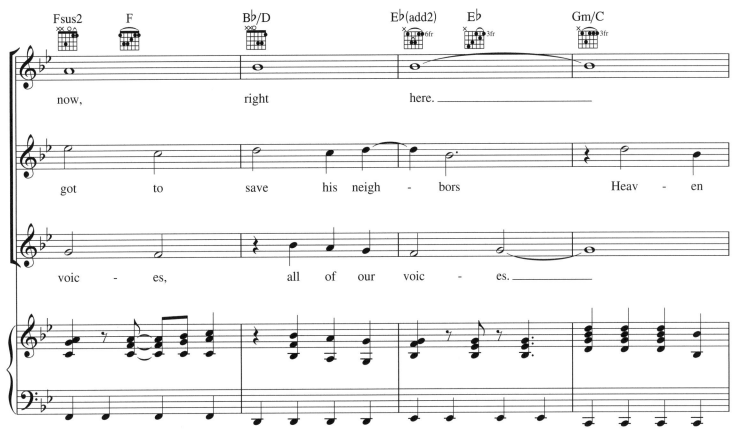

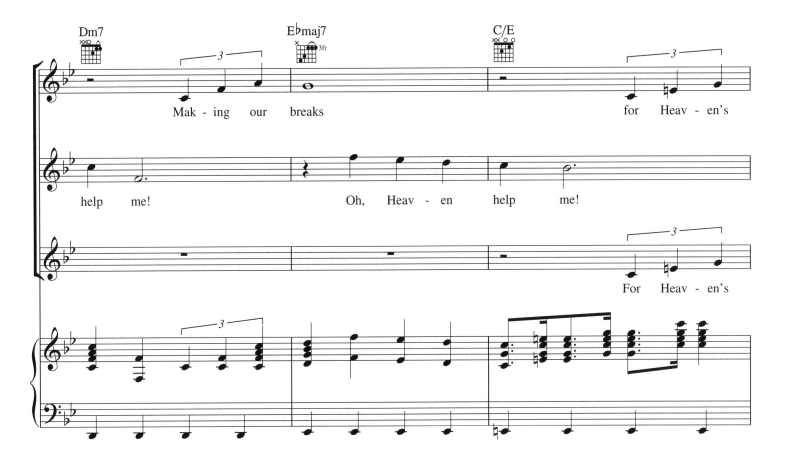

LET'S HEAR IT FOR THE BOY

Words by DEAN PITCHFORD
Music by TOM SNOW

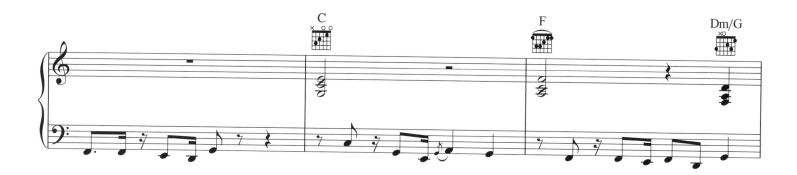

RUSTY:

My

ba - by, he don't talk sweet; — he ain't got much to

Recorded a whole step higher.

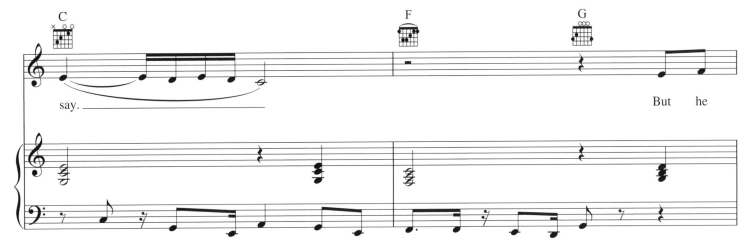

say. _____ But he

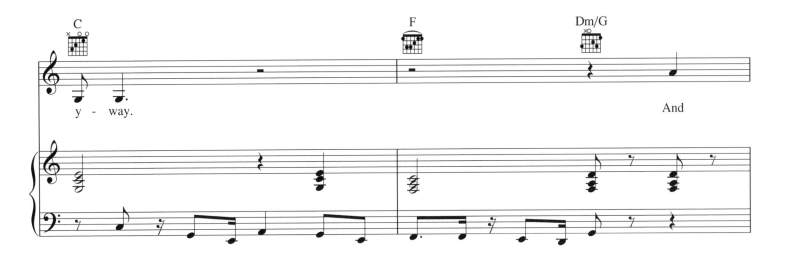

loves me, loves _ me, loves ___ me. I know that he loves me an -

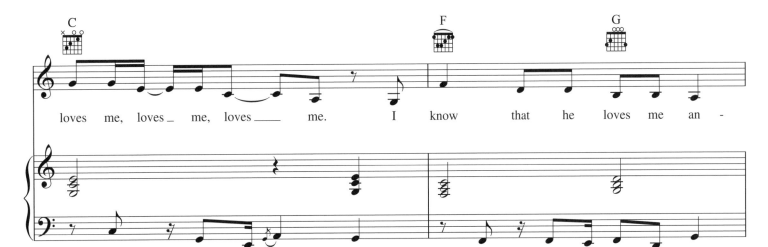

y - way. And

may - be he don't dress fine, __ but I don't real - ly

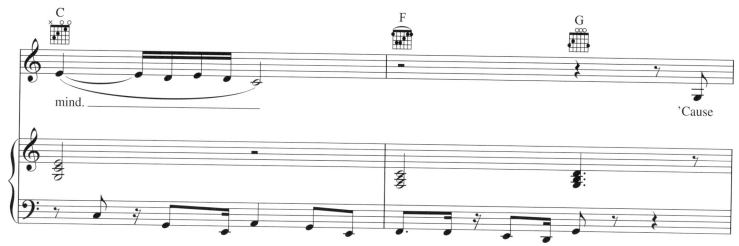

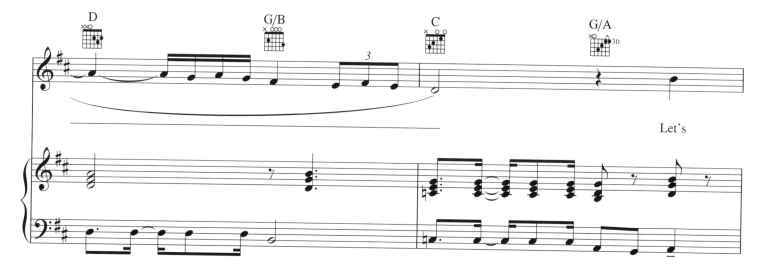

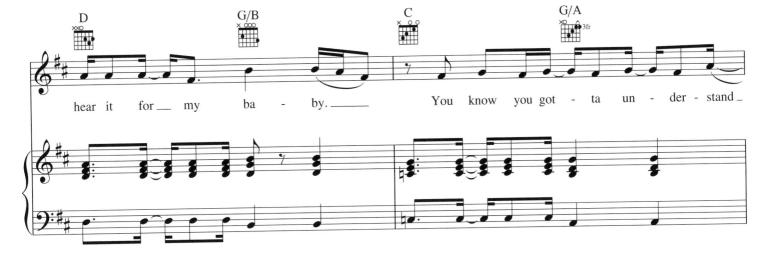

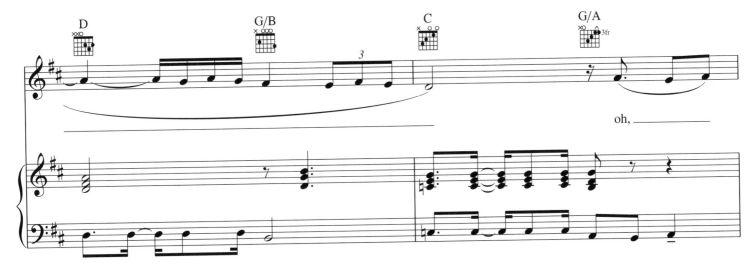

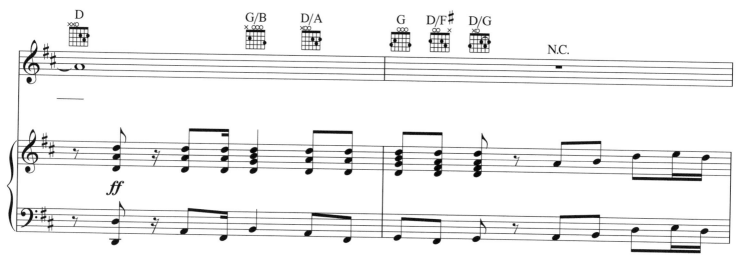

My

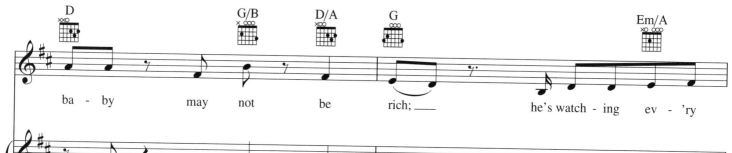

ba - by may not be rich; ___ he's watch - ing ev - 'ry

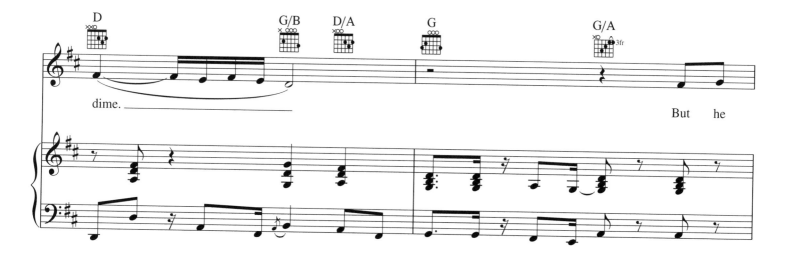

dime. ___

But he

loves me, loves _ me, loves ____ me, and we al - ways have _ a real ____ good ____

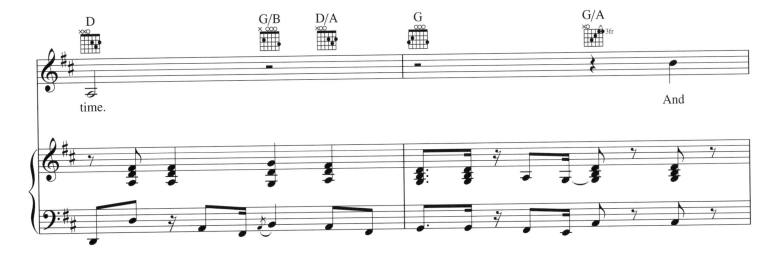

time. And

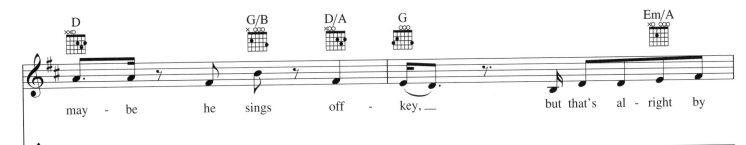

may - be he sings off - key, ___ but that's al - right by

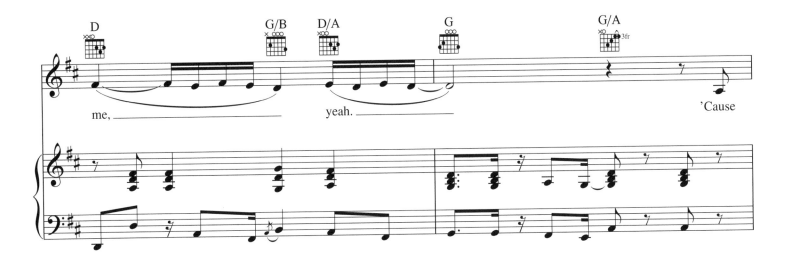

me, _____ yeah. _____ 'Cause

what he does __ he does so well, makes me want to yell. __ Let's

hear it for __ the boy! __ Let's give the boy __ a hand. __

Let's

hear it for __ my ba - by. You know you got - ta un - der - stand. __

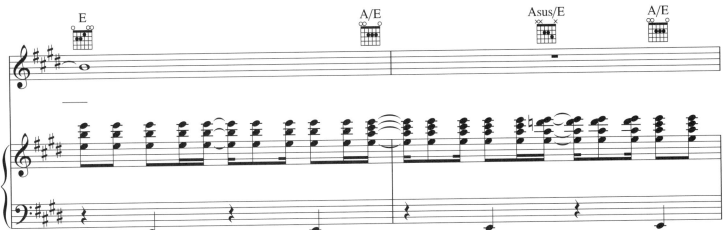

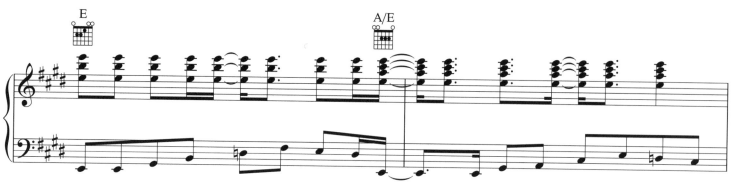

Maybe he's no Cas-a-no-va; still, his kiss-es knock me o-ver.

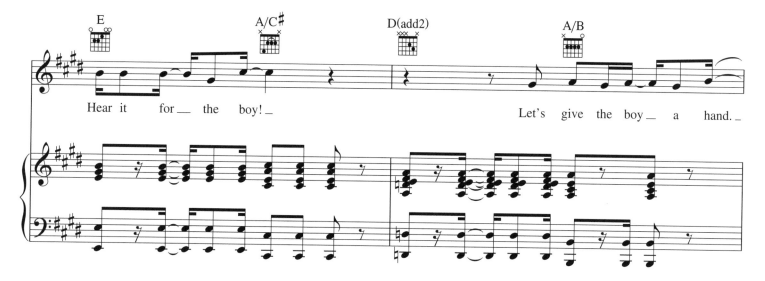

Hear it for the boy! Let's give the boy a hand.

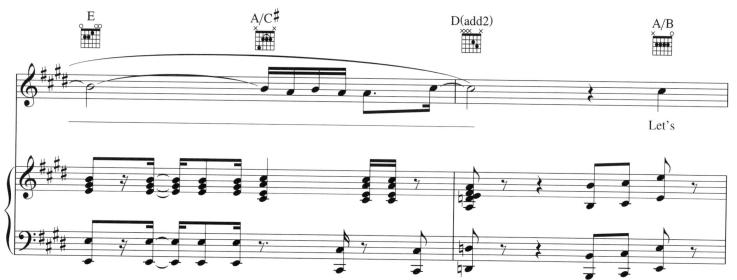

Let's

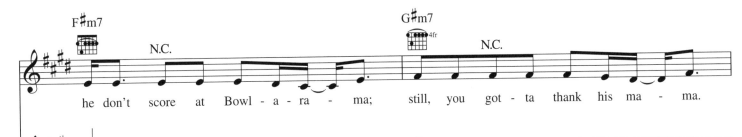

SOMEBODY'S EYES

Words by DEAN PITCHFORD
Music by TOM SNOW

Tense and precise

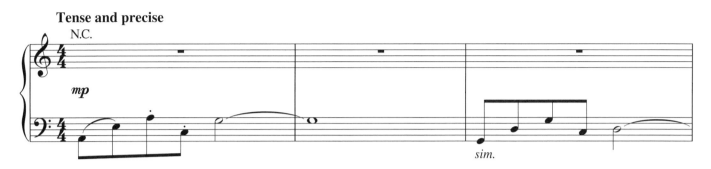

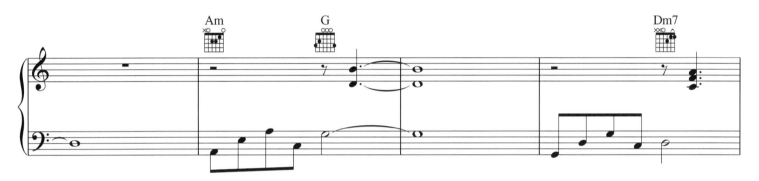

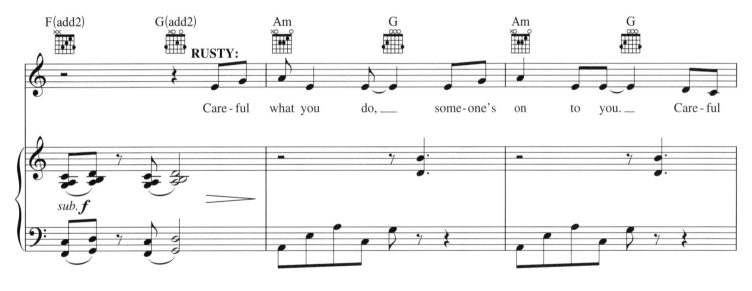

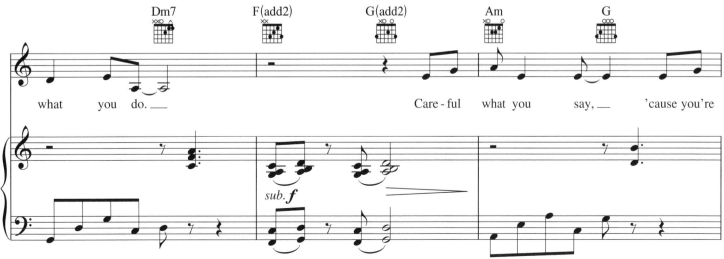

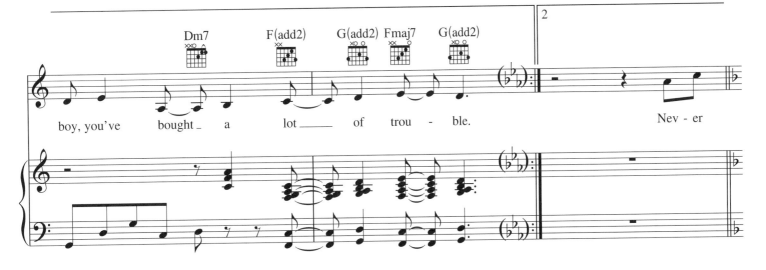

boy, you've bought _ a lot ___ of trou - ble.   Nev - er

laugh too loud, _ nev - er leave a crowd, _ nev - er dress ris - qué, _ there'll be

hell to pay. _ If you've ev - er had ___ an - y-thing to hide, _

think twice be - fore you step out - side. ___

MAMA SAYS

Words by DEAN PITCHFORD
Music by TOM SNOW

Ma - ma makes _ a lot - ta sense, if you know how to lis - ten. She is

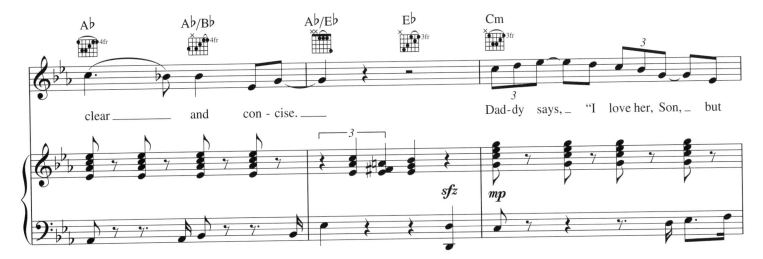

clear _____ and con - cise. _____ Dad - dy says, _ "I love her, Son, _ but

she's got mar - bles miss - in'." But I say, "Hey! _ It's

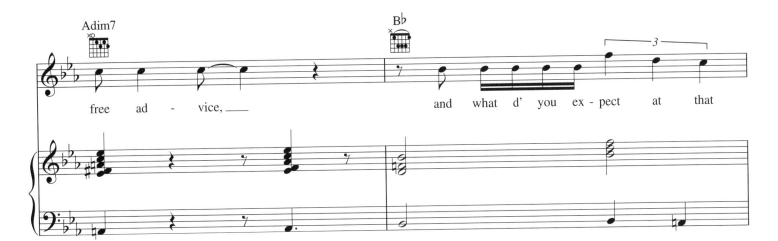

free ad - vice, _____ and what d' you ex - pect at that

Once you drive up a moun - tain, you can't back

down. Once you drive up a moun-tain, you

can't back down!

ON ANY SUNDAY

Words by DEAN PITCHFORD
Music by TOM SNOW

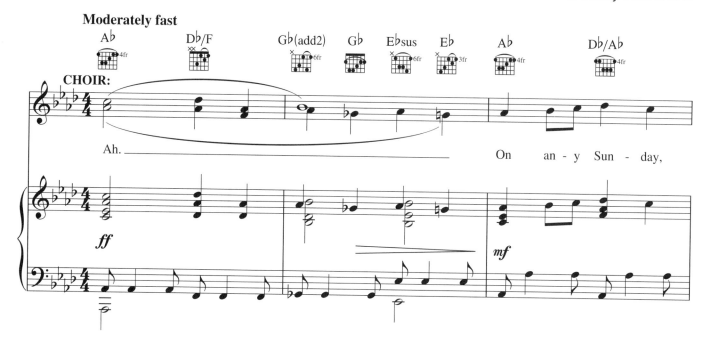

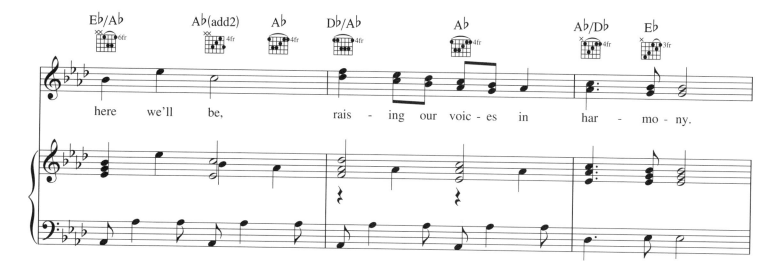

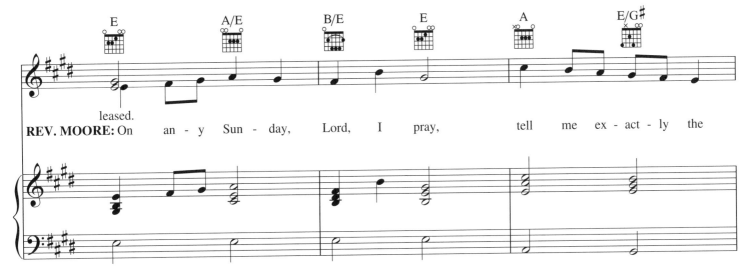

leased.

REV. MOORE: On an-y Sun-day, Lord, I pray, tell me ex-act-ly the

words to say. Give me strength, and may-be then

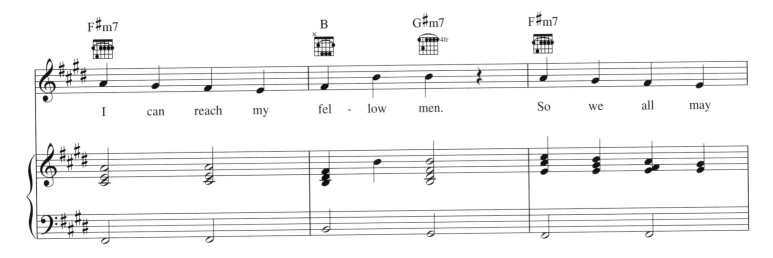

I can reach my fel-low men. So we all may

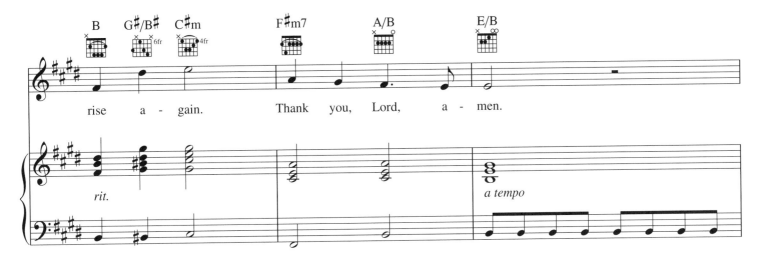

rise a-gain. Thank you, Lord, a-men.

rit.

a tempo

REN:
We've on-ly been here two days and al-read-y Chi-

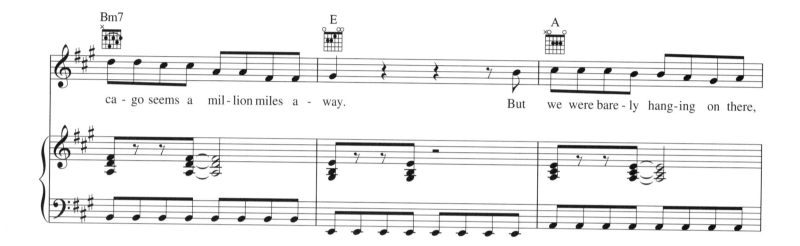

ca-go seems a mil-lion miles a-way. But we were bare-ly hang-ing on there,

'spe-cial-ly with my fa-ther gone. There's not too man-y plac-es we could

stay. But may-be Mom could find a job that's stead-y, and

may-be I could stand it for a year, and may-be things won't be so bad, and

may-be I won't miss my dad, and may-be we could start a new life here.

CHOIR:
Ah, _____

start a new life here.

mp delicately

The right thing, the right thing.

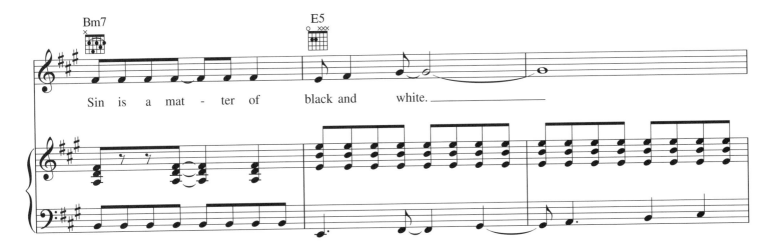

Sin is a mat - ter of black and white. ___

KIDS:

There's ru - mors go - in' 'round a - bout the new kid, and

ev - 'ry - bod - y's talk - in' 'til they're blue. 'Cause you know how a stran - ger is, if

he's not dumb, he's dan-ger-ous, but ei-ther way, at least it's some-thing new.

REV. MOORE, VI, ARIEL:

God is love.

Fol - low Him and nev - er

roam. He has made the stars

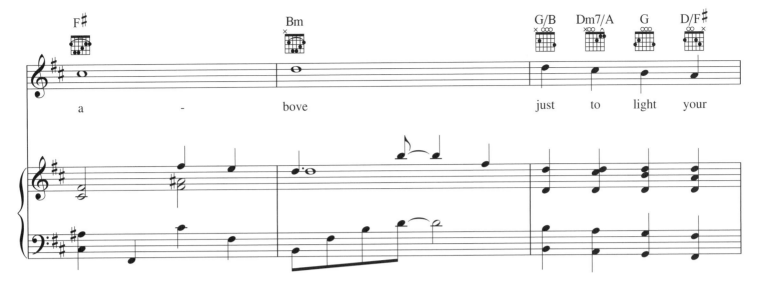

a - bove   just to light your

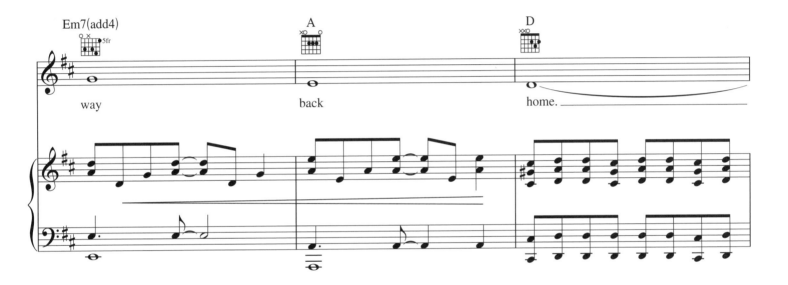

way   back   home.

CHOIR:
The   right thing,   the   right thing.   We

REV. MOORE,
PARISHIONERS:
God   is

ETHEL, REN*:
We've   on - ly been here two days and al - read - y   Chi -

*Ren's part in the same octave, as written.

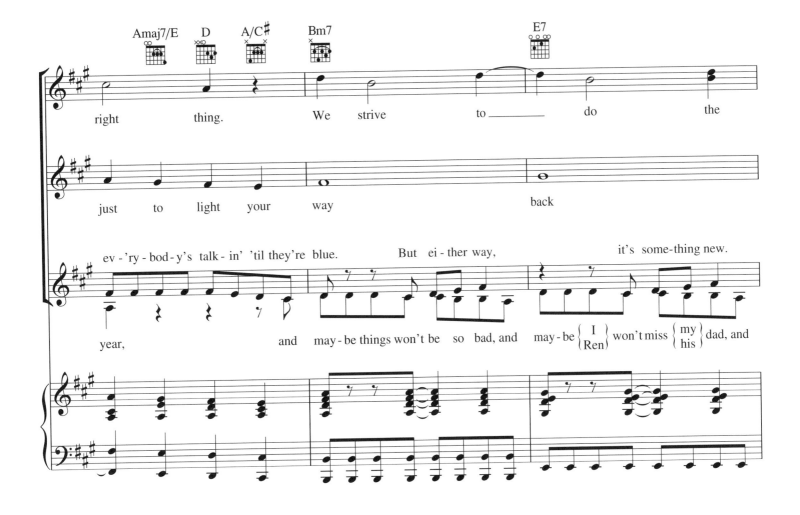

right ____ thing. ____ On an-y Sun-day morn-ing, here __

home. ____

Ei-ther way, at least it's some-thing new.

may-be we can start a new life here.

joyful

__ we'll be, __ rais-ing our voic-es in har - mo-ny,

STILL ROCKIN'

Words by DEAN PITCHFORD
Music by TOM SNOW

COWBOY BOB:
Woke up in the day-light, don't re-mem-ber last night. I just know I was-n't a-lone.

I par-tied in the fast lane, I was feel-in' no pain.

Some-bod - y car - ried me home. ____ Now I kick ____ off the sheets, run ____

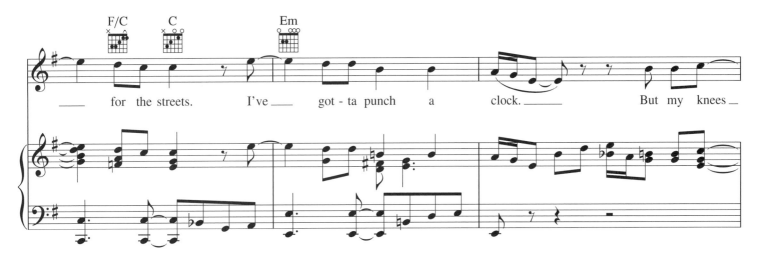

____ for the streets. I've ____ got - ta punch a clock. ____ But my knees ____

____ are go - ing one way— Whoo! and my feet ____ won't ____ stop. Gim-

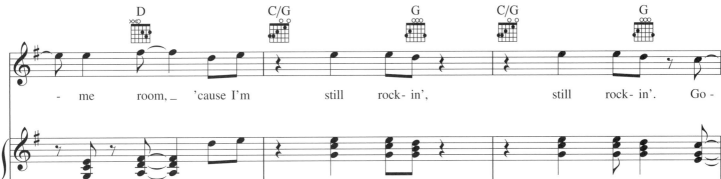

- me room, ____ 'cause I'm still rock - in', still rock - in'. Go-

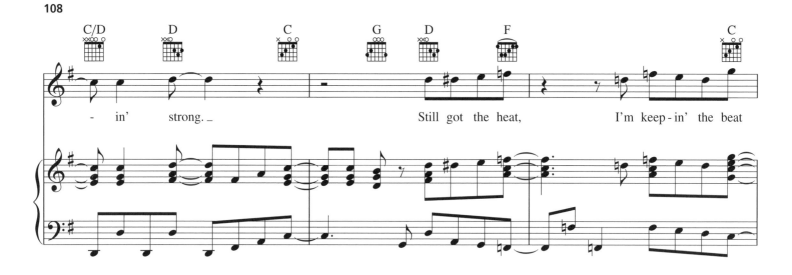

- in' strong. ___ Still got the heat, I'm keep-in' the beat

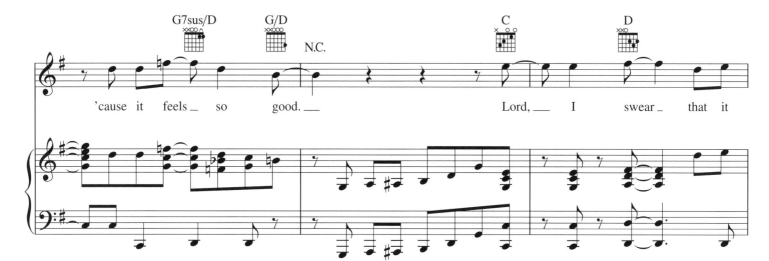

'cause it feels ___ so good. ___ Lord, ___ I swear ___ that it

beats walk-in'. I'm still rock-in' all ___ day long. ___

Shak-in' my shoes, ___ I'm spread-in' the news that I'm feel-in' so good. ___

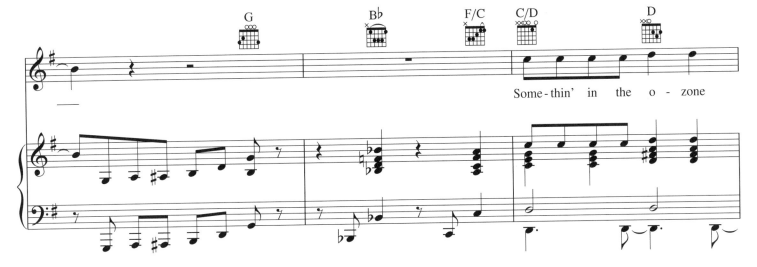

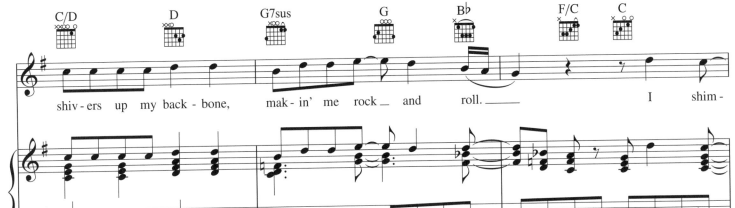

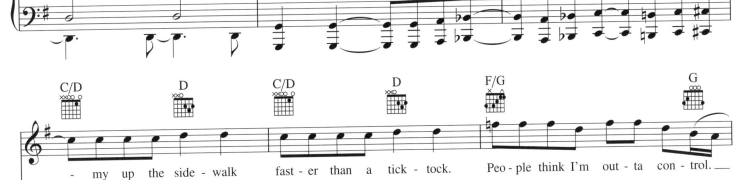

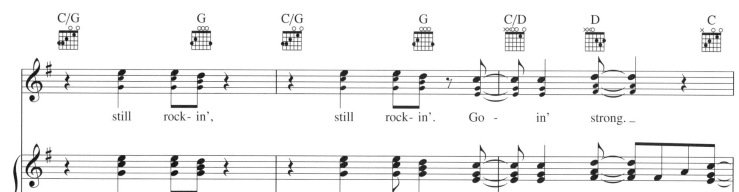

Lord, __ I swear __ that it beats walk-in'.

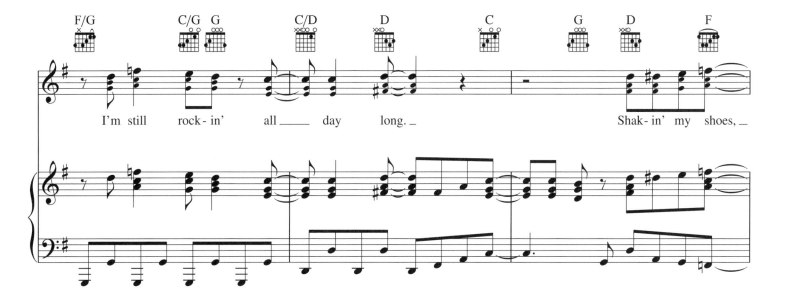

I'm still rock-in' all ___ day long. __ Shak-in' my shoes, __

__ I'm spread-in' the news that I'm feel-in' so good. __

BAND:

Lord, __